THE BIBLE IN WORKSHEETS

Conway Dunn

 en Press

Copyright© Conway Dunn 2011

All rights reserved

No part of this publication may be reproduced,
stored in a retrieval system, or transmitted
in any form or by any means, without
the prior permission in writing of the publisher,
nor be otherwise circulated in any form of binding or cover other than that in
which it is published and without a similar condition including this condition
being imposed on the subsequent purchaser.

First published in Great Britain by Pen Press

Pen Press is an imprint of Indepenpress Publishing Ltd
25 Eastern Place
Brighton
BN2 1GJ

ISBN 13: 978-1-78003-030-2

All paper used in the printing of this book has been made from wood grown in
managed, sustainable forests.

Printed and bound in the UK

A catalogue record of this book is available from
the British Library

Cover design by Jacqueline Abromeit

The Author

Conway Dunn taught Religious Studies for over twenty years in a variety of schools, to ages ranging from eight to eighteen.
He is the author of the essays, *'One Man's Thoughts'*.

****

Acknowledgements

My gratitude to my wife, Agatha,
for her assistance in the preparation of this book.

Contents

THE BIBLE	1
TimeLine	5
THE OLD TESTAMENT	7
The Creation	9
Sin	11
Noah	14
The Tower of Babel	17
Abraham	19
Joseph	21
Moses	24
The Ten Commandments	28
The Conquest of Canaan	30
Saul	32
David	36
Solomon	39
Isaiah	42
Ezekiel	44
The Return	47
Daniel	49
Old Testament Crossword	51
THE NEW TESTAMENT	55
The Gospels	57
The Nativity	58
Childhood, Baptism and Temptations	61
The Disciples	64
Teachings	67
Miracles	71
The Closing Stages	75

The Last Supper, the Arrest and the Trial before the High Priest	77
The Trial before Pilate, the Crucifixion and the Burial	81
The Resurrection	84
Post-resurrection Appearances and the Ascension	86
The Early Church	88
The Letters	93
Revelation	95
New Testament Crossword	98
NOTES	
Taxation	105
The Sanhedrin	106
The Pharisees	106
The Sadducees	106
The Scribes	106
Judas Iscariot	107
The Messiah	109
The Temples in Jerusalem	110
Synagogues (meeting-places)	114
Illness (in biblical times)	115
Sacrifices – Offerings to God	116
QUIZ	117

The Bible

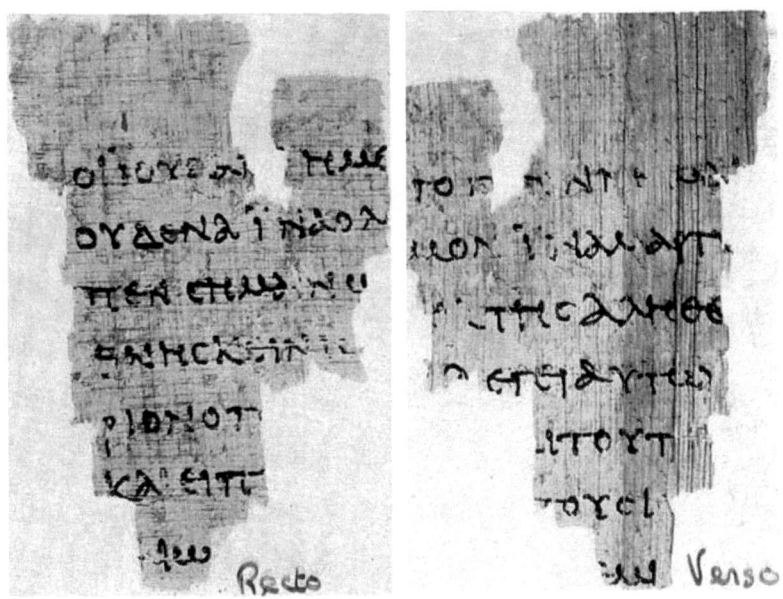

Fragment of St John's gospel written in the early 2nd century (130–150)

Read the following, filling in the blanks:

The Bible, meaning 'collection of writings', contains ------- separate books, split into two sections, The --------- Testament and The ------------ Testament, the first consisting of --------- books and the second of --------. Each book is divided into c----- and, further, into v--------.

These books, written over a period of about one thousand years, begin with God and the universe (the creation), then they concentrate on God's relationship with one race in particular, the ---------, but the books end returning to God's plans for the whole world (the new creation).

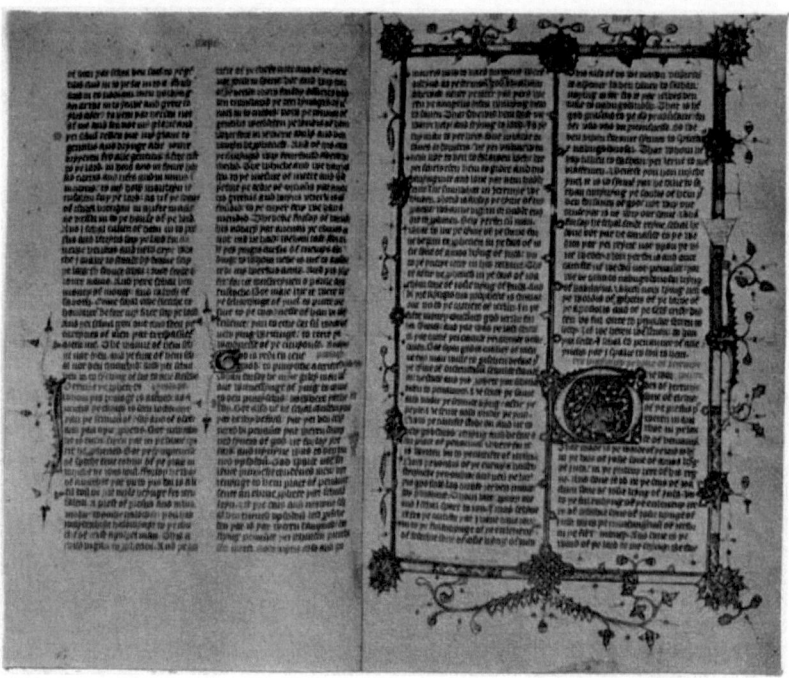

Two pages from the first English translation of the Bible in the 14th century

Answer the following:

1) Name the first book and the last in the Bible

2) Which book has the most chapters?

3) Which book has the least chapters?

4) Roughly, how much of the Bible is occupied by The Old Testament, ¾, ⅔ or ½?

5) What is the Pentateuch?

6) What are the Gospels?

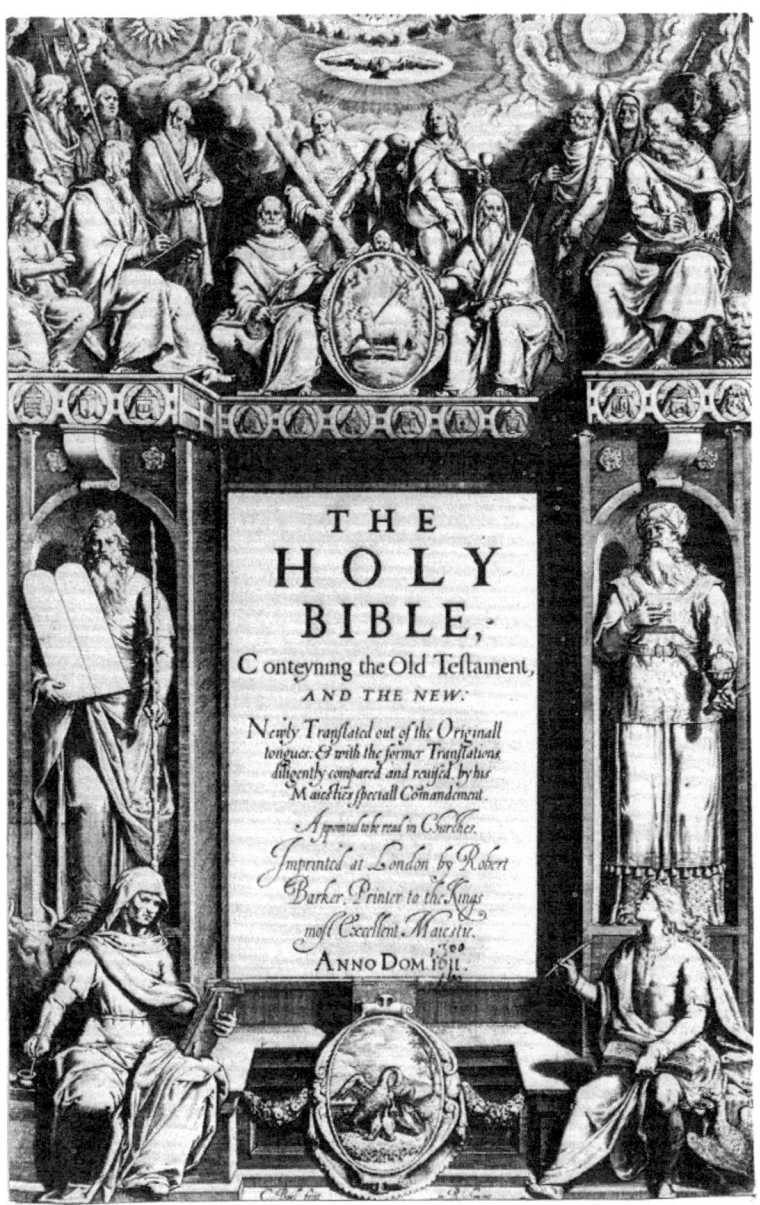

Cover of the first edition of the Authorised version of the Bible (King James'), 1611.

Timeline B.C. (Before Christ)

c. = about   C = century

c. C 19th	Abraham
c. C 17th	Joseph
c. C 13th	Moses. The exodus The conquest of Canaan.
c. C 12th and C 11th	The rule of the Judges
c. 1020 – 1000	The reign of Saul
c. 1000 – 960	The reign of David
c. 960 – 920	The reign of Solomon
Two kingdoms	Israel and Judah
c. 720	Assyrian conquest Isaiah
c. 600	Babylonian conquest Ezekiel
c. 540	Persian conquest
c. 330	Greek conquest
c. C 2nd	Daniel
c. 60	Roman conquest

THE

OLD

TESTAMENT

The Creation

'In the beginning…'

The Old Testament begins with the story of the Creation

1.a. Read Genesis ch.1 v.'s 1 and 2.
  b. Did God create the universe out of something or out of nothing?
2. Genesis ch.1 has one account of creation; Genesis ch.2 another.
  a. Make a list of the order of creation in each account.
  b. What similarities can you find?
     The two accounts differ in style – the first reads like a list; the second, like a story.
  c. How does God differ in the two accounts, e.g. in the first, he commands; in the second, he makes?

Where the Rivers Tigris and Euphrates meet, in Iraq. Read Gen. ch.2 v.'s 10–14.

3. In the Bible there is mention of God overcoming monsters – two, in particular, Leviathan (see Psalm 74, v.'s 12–17) and Rahab (see Isaiah ch.51 v.9). Perhaps they threatened the creation.
   The Babylonians had such a story – their gods were opposed by monsters
   a. For a vivid description of Leviathan read Job ch.41.
   b. Draw a picture of him, based on this reading.

4. Today many people believe that life began with a chemical reaction and species (types) evolved from (developed out of) others, over millions of years.
   One version of this theory is:

   ```
   5,000m*–500m:   life began
   500m–300m:      sea-life only.
        300m:      amphibians emerged
        200m:      reptiles emerged
         75m:      mammals emerged
              m*= millions of years
   ```

   a. How did the chemicals come to exist?
   b. How did anything come to exist?

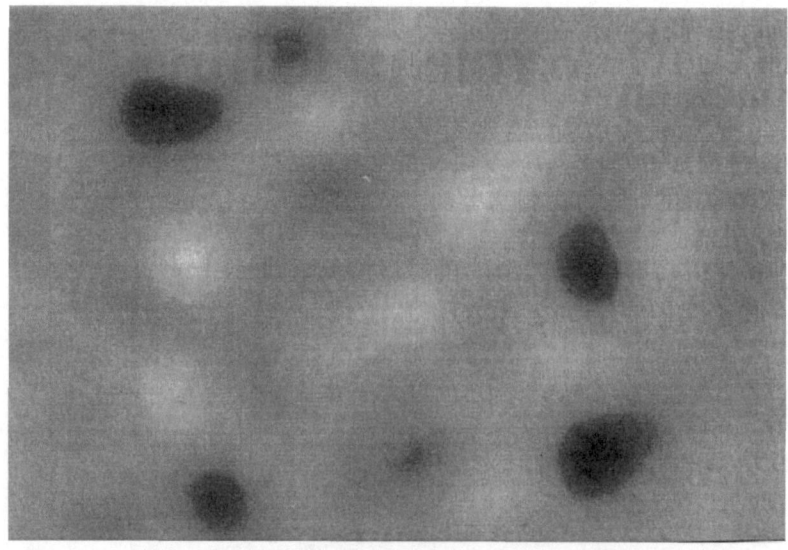

'In the beginning…' according to scientists. The picture is of distant space, the patches showing slight differences of temperature, caused by the differences of density between energy and matter which, coming together, form galaxies.

Sin

Genesis ch.3 tells the story of man's disobedience and God's punishments – how sin and suffering came into the world.

1 a. Read Genesis ch.3 v.'s 1–13.

   b. Write the account as a play. The characters are the snake, the woman, God and the man. Keep the meanings of their words, but express them in your own words.

   c. The man blamed the woman. The woman blamed the snake. Can you think of a situation where someone's reaction to an accusation has been to blame someone else?

   d. Why did God allow the snake – sometimes seen as the devil – to threaten his blissful creation?

2 a. Read Genesis ch.3 v.'s 14–19.

   b. Summarise the punishments on:

      (i) The snake.

      (ii) The woman.

      (iii) The man.

3. It seems that Adam and Eve could choose to eat or not to eat the fruit. They had free-will.

   a. How free are we in our choices? How far are we affected by factors such as our backgrounds? If, for example, we grow up in a family with certain beliefs, how difficult is it for us not to have those beliefs?

'Adam and Eve' by Lucas Cranach the Elder

'The expulsion from Eden' by Masaccio

Noah

Sin spread so much that God decided to destroy life, but one man, Noah, was good.

1a. Read from Gen. ch.6 v.5 to ch.9 v.17. Notice the story ends with an explanation for the rainbow.

  b. Read the following, filling in the blanks:

     God told Noah to make an ark, about----- long, ----- wide and ----- high. ----- people and ----- of every animal and bird boarded the ark.

     The flood came. It rained for ----- days. All the land was submerged. Everything not on the ark was killed.

     The water began to go down. The ark grounded on Mt -----.

     Later, Noah sent out a ----- and a ----- to see if they could find any dry land. Eventually the ----- returned with an ----- leaf.

     About ----- days after the flood began, the earth was dry. Everyone left the ark.

     God made a covenant that never again would a flood destroy all life. The covenant had a sign: a ----- .

  c. What is a covenant?

2. Draw a diagram of the ark, based on the information given in Gen. ch.6. Write, around it, the measurements.

3. The Babylonians also had a flood story:

     The gods decided to destroy mankind because men were too noisy. But one god warned a man called Utnapishtim. The god told him to build a boat and take on it "the seed of all living creatures." Utnapishtim made a boat about 180 feet square, and went on board with his family, craftsmen and animals.

     A great storm broke, and continued for a week. All men, except those on board, were killed. The boat grounded on Mt Nisir. A week later Utnapishtim released a dove and a swallow, but finding no resting-place, they returned. He sent out a raven and she did not come back.

     He opened the boat and made a sacrifice. The gods smelt it and gathered like flies. Utnapishtim was made immortal.

Write down some of the similarities and differences between this story and the one in Genesis.

A Babylonian version of the flood, inscribed on a clay tablet.

4. "The boat came to rest on a mountain in the Ararat range." (Gen. ch.8 v.4). Agri Dagi, in Turkey, now known as Mt Ararat, has been the focal point.

Mt Ararat

From the time of the Middle Ages, at least, there have been reports of an ark on this mountain, and various expeditions claim to have found one, intact. In 1955 a Frenchman brought down some wood, possibly from the boat, which was radio-carbon dated, but the date revealed was the C.8th A.D.

Recently, a flat, boat-like shape, about the size of the ark, has been found on ground twenty miles from Mt Ararat (see picture overleaf).

Imagine you were searching for the ark. Tell your story.

5. A problem:

   Why did God destroy not only "these people", but "also the animals and the birds" (Gen. ch.6 v.7)?

THE REMAINS OF NOAH'S ARK?

The Tower of Babel (Babylon)

1 a. Read Gen. ch.11 v.'s 1–9.

   b. Why did the people build a tower?

   c. The story explains why people speak different languages. What followed from this event?

2. Draw a rough outline of the world and mark on it as many languages as you can.

3. "The tower" might have been inspired by ziggurats, buildings constructed in layers, each smaller than the one below, with a temple at the top.

A diagram:

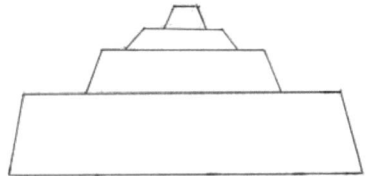

There was a ziggurat at Ur, in Babylonia, about 300 feet square and 300 feet high.

The remains of the ziggurat at Ur

Some steps of the ziggurat

4. Why did people like to worship from a high spot, such as the top of a hill or a building?

Abraham

Abraham (known, at first, as Abram) lived around 2,000 B.C. God called him saying that he would have many descendants and they would become a nation. God would be their god.

1. Read Gen. ch.12 v.'s 1–7 and Gen. ch.17 v.'s 1–14.

2. Abraham was brought up at Ur (in Babylonia). He moved to Haran (in Mesopotamia) and then to Shechem (in Canaan).

   Find these places on a map.

3. Why did "Abram" become "Abraham"?

4. What was the physical sign of the covenant God made with Abraham?

5. Abraham's faith was tested.

   a. Read Gen. ch.22 v.'s 1–19.

   b. Write the story imagining that you were Isaac.

The rock, now inside a mosque, in Jerusalem, where Abraham almost sacrificed Isaac.

6. From the passages read, write down six things God said he would do for Abraham.

The tomb of Abraham, in Hebron

Joseph

Jacob (later named Israel), a grandson of Abraham, had twelve sons and he loved one, Joseph, more than the others. Because of this, the other brothers hated Joseph and sold him into slavery. He was taken to Egypt where he rose to become "prime minister".

He forgave his brothers and invited the whole family to join him. So the Israelites moved to Egypt.

1. Why was Jacob's name changed to Israel? Read Gen. ch.32 v.'s 22–32.
2. a. Read the story of Joseph from Gen. ch.37 v.1 – ch.47 v.12.
   b. Who was to blame for the bad-feeling in the family?

An ancient Egyptian manuscript listing good and bad dreams and their interpretations.

   c. Make a comic-strip account of Joseph's family coming to Egypt (Gen. ch.42 onwards).

Divide a page into eight squares. Write headings for the squares as follows:

1) Brothers come to buy corn.
2) Jos. accuses them of spying.
3) Imprisons Simeon. Demands Benjamin.
4) Jacob, reluctantly, lets Ben. go.
5) Jos. hides cup in Ben's sack.
6) Judah's speech
7) Jos. reveals himself. Invitation.
8) Jacob and family come and settle.

Draw pictures of each heading; include (where it helps) "bubble" speech, as in a comic.

  d. What do you think of the tricks Joseph played on his brothers when they came to buy corn?

Painting, in an Egyptian tomb, of a harvest

3. Joseph's life had "ups" and "downs". Using the diagram below – a distorted W – to show this, fill in the missing words:

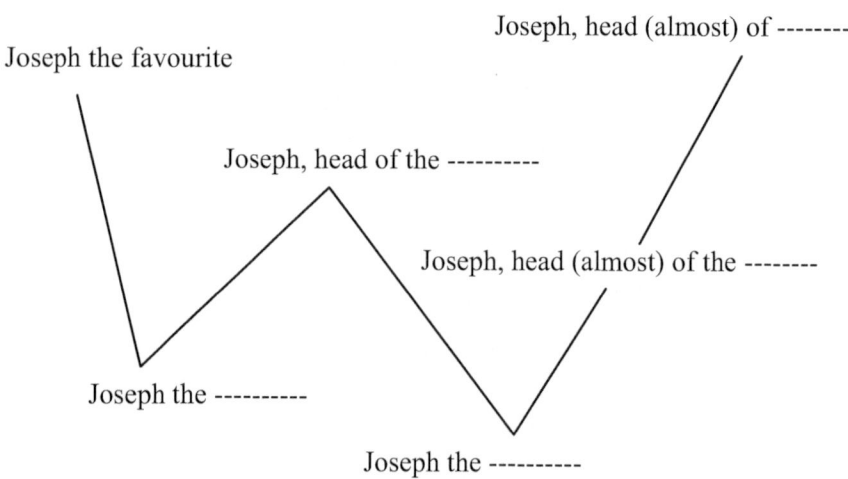

Joseph the favourite

Joseph, head (almost) of ----------

Joseph, head of the ----------

Joseph, head (almost) of the --------

Joseph the ----------

Joseph the ----------

The story of Joseph teaches that the person who has God on their side will overcome setbacks and triumph – "…the Lord was with Joseph and made him succeed in everything he did" (Gen. ch.39 v.23)

**Model of an Egyptian official, c. 1500B.C.
Joseph probably dressed in a similar fashion.**

Moses

In Egypt the Israelites became numerous. A new pharaoh regarded them as a threat. So he made them slaves. An Israelite called Moses fled to the land of Midian.

One day God told Moses to return to Egypt and lead his people to the country of Canaan, "the promised land" (see Gen. ch.17 v.'s 7, 8).

1. a. Read Exodus ch.3 v.'s 1–10.

   b. What does "exodus" mean?

2. Moses raised objections, including, what was God's name? What name did God say? Read Exodus ch.3 v.'s 14, 15.

   The name developed as follows:
   Y H W H – I AM – Y A H WE H – J E H 0 V A H – THE LORD.

Moses returned to Egypt, but pharaoh would not let the people go. So God sent plagues upon the Egyptians; the one that made the king give in was called "The Passover".

It is thought that the pharaoh who ruled during the exodus was Rameses II (c. 1291 – 1224).

A statue of Rameses II

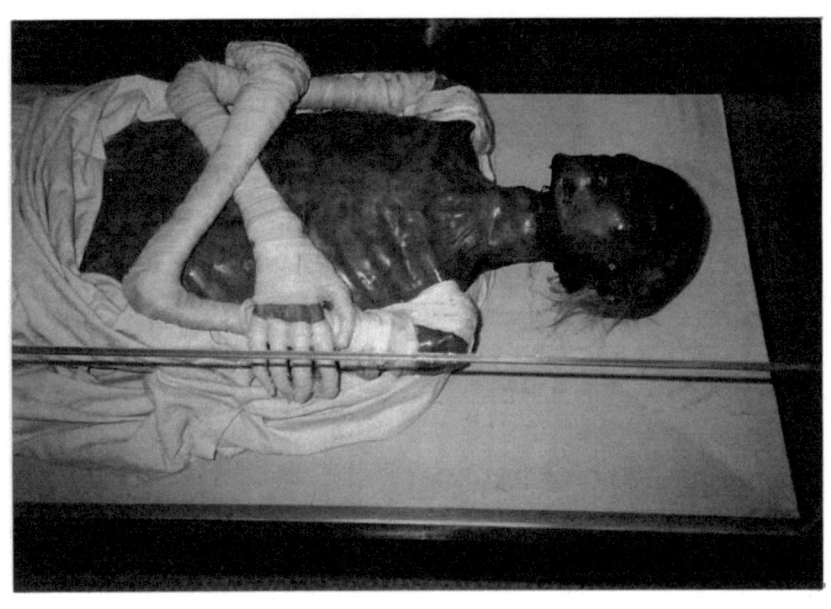

His mummified remains

3. a. Read Exodus ch.12 v.'s 1–40.

   b. Do the Passover crossword.

Across

1. What God did (6, 4)
3. Those to be killed (5,4)
5. The age of the animal to be killed (3,4)
7. The type of bread eaten (10)
9. The city the Israelites set out from (7)
11. The Passover was to be remembered for all ---- (4)
13. The day the animal was chosen (5)
15. What the Israelites were to be dressed for (6)
17. What was used to smear the blood (6)
19. About how many hundred thousand men left Egypt? (3)
21. The Passover honoured the ---- (4)

Down

2. How the meat was to be cooked (7)
4. The day the animal was killed (10)
6. The country the Israelites set out from (5)
8. What the blood was smeared around (5)
10. How many days the festival of Unleavened Bread was to last for (5)
12. Have it to hand whilst eating (5)
14. The gender of the animal the Israelites were to kill (4)
16. How the Egyptians would ask the Israelites to leave (3)
18. Pharaoh's relation who died (3)
20. One of the Egyptians' possessions given to the Israelites (4)
22. The Israelites had lived in Egypt for over ---- hundred years (4)
24. They left at ....(5)

Answers to Passover Crossword

Across

1. Passed over
3. First-born
5. One-year
7. Unleavened
9. Rameses
11. Time
13. Tenth
15. Travel
17. Hyssop
19. Six
21. Lord

Down

2. Roasted
4. Fourteenth
6. Egypt
8. Doors
10. Seven
12. Stick
14. Male
16. Beg
18. Son
20. Gold
22. Four
24. Night

The Ten Commandments

The Israelites set out for "the promised land". During the journey God gave Moses many laws; ten are particularly well-known, and they are called "The Ten Commandments".

Mt Sinai, where Moses received "The Ten Commandments"

1. a. Read Exodus ch.20 v.'s 1–17.

   b. How many commands are about how people should treat God?

   c. How many are about how people should treat each other?

2. Are any of these commands in the laws of every country, so far as you know? Discuss

3. Think of 10 commandments for today.

   Write them down, then draw them as signs, e.g. Don't drop litter.

4. Learn this poem:

> Have thou no other gods but me,
> And to no image bow thy knee.
> Take not the name of God in vain:
> The Sabbath day do not profane.
> Honour thy father and mother too;
> And see that thou no murder do.
> Abstain from words and deeds unclean;
> Nor steal, though thou art poor and mean.
> Bear not false witness, shun that blot;
> What is thy neighbour's covet not.
>
> (Anonymous. 1731)

The Conquest of Canaan

The Israelites reached the land of Canaan. They crossed the River Jordan which, like the Red Sea, parted miraculously.

1. a. Read Joshua ch.3 v.'s 14–17.

    b. Later, two prophets also parted the river. Who were they?
       Read 2 Kings ch.2 v.'s 8, 14.

Under their new leader, Joshua, the people of Israel attacked the Canaanites.

2.   The city of Jericho, also, was overcome miraculously.

    a. Read Joshua ch.6.

    b. Write down the different parts of the procession that marched around the city.

    c. Imagine you were in some way involved in the battle. Describe your experience.

    d. Apart from Rahab and her household, everyone and every animal in Jericho was killed, and the city was burnt. Read Joshua ch.6 v.'s 17, 21, 24. What do you think about this?

The ruins of Jericho

The Israelites spread out and dominated Canaan. They divided the land between their tribes. Quite often, a leader of national importance emerged, usually to fight against an invader – such a leader was Samson.

1. Read Judges ch.'s 13, 14, 15 and 16.
2. Samson was a nazirite. Find out how a nazirite showed that he was dedicated to God.
3. To what extent were women responsible for Samson's misfortunes? To what extent was he himself responsible? Discuss.

So long as Samson's hair was uncut – so long as he was a nazirite – he demonstrated great strength. When his hair was cut – when he stopped being a nazirite – he was no stronger than a normal person.

Behind this strange notion may lie a religious message: so long as people obey God, he helps them and they are successful; if they do not obey God, he does not help them and they fail.

Another message would be, disobedience will be punished. Prophet after prophet made this point; it was an explanation for the country being repeatedly conquered.

4. Read, for example:

   a. 1 Samuel ch.12 v.9.

   b. Jeremiah ch.6 v.'s 18, 19, 22, 23.

   c. Hosea ch.8 v.'s 1–3

   d. Amos ch.6 v.'s 12, 14

   e. Micah ch.1 v.'s 5, 9.

   f. Habakkuk ch.1 v.'s 2–6, 12.

   g. Zechariah ch. 7 v.'s 8–14.

Saul

The people of Israel wanted a king. They chose Saul. He drove back the Philistines, and defeated other surrounding enemies, but he soon lost the (grudging) support of Samuel, the prophet and former leader.

1. a. Read 1 Samuel ch.10 v.8 and ch.13 v.'s 5–14, and 1 Samuel ch.15.

   b. Was it fair that Saul was rejected for these reasons?

   c. Was Samuel still trying to be the leader?

Ramah, Samuel's home

Samuel turned to David as the new king, though Saul was still on the throne. David entered Saul's service, as a musician and as a soldier. He was befriended by the king's son, Jonathan.

David defeated the giant, Goliath.

2. a. Read 1 Samuel ch.17. v.'s 1–54.

   b. Draw your own picture of Goliath, and mark on it his height, and the weight of his armour and of his spear's head.

   c. Who killed Goliath according to 2 Samuel ch.21 v.19?

The valley of Elah

In battle David was so successful that Saul feared that he would become king. So Saul tried to kill him, then changed his mind, then tried again. Eventually David fled and lived as an outlaw, still pursued by the king.

3. Imagine you were an outlaw. How would you have survived from day to day?
   Compare your answers to 1 Samuel ch.22 v.'s 1, 2; ch.25 v.'s 2–13; ch. 27 v.'s 1, 2.

The region of Engedi, by the Dead Sea, where David hid from Saul

Once again the Philistines attacked. Saul asked a medium (a person who claims to make contact with the spirits of the dead) what would happen.

4. a. Read 1 Samuel ch.28 v.'s 4–19.

   b. Write a short play of this event.

The battle took place. Saul was badly wounded and rather than be captured he committed suicide.

Beth Shan, where the Philistines took Saul's body and nailed it to the wall of the city.

5. Was Saul "a man more sinn'd against than sinning" (Shakespeare, from 'King Lear', Act 3, Scene 2)? Discuss

David

David became king, first of Judah, the southern region, then of all Israel.

1. He captured the city of Jerusalem and made it the capital of the country.
   a. Read 2 Samuel ch.5 v.'s 6–9.
   b. From this passage, and from your own research, suggest reasons why David chose this city in particular as the capital.

2. He moved Israel's most sacred religious possession, the Covenant Box, to Jerusalem, so making the city the religious, as well as the political, capital.
   a. Read Exodus ch.25 v.'s 10, 11.
   b. Draw a diagram of the Covenant Box.
   c. What was placed inside it? Read Exodus ch.25 v.16.

An original pathway to the city of David, Jerusalem

3. David defeated the Philistines, the old enemy. He conquered the lands of Moab, Edom, Ammon and southern Syria, thereby giving Israel an empire.

   a. Find these countries on a map and compare the size of Israel before and after their inclusion. How much larger, roughly, does the territory become? Double? Triple? Quadruple?

4. Should a person be admired because they conquer other nations?

5. During the war against the Ammonites, David took another man's wife: he made sure Uriah, a soldier, was killed in battle and then he married Uriah's widow, Bathsheba. Nathan the prophet told a story:

   a. Read 2 Samuel ch.12 v.'s 1–4.

   b. Nathan said David was like the rich man. Who was like the poor man? Who was like the poor man's lamb?

   c. As punishment, David would suffer, and so would many of his relatives, including some of his descendants, in every generation. Is this fair? Consider Exodus ch.34 v.7.

   d. Read 2 Samuel ch.12 v.11. David's son, Absalom, rebelled against him. What did David do? Read 2 Samuel ch.15 v.'s 13–16. There was a battle. What happened to Absalom? Read 2 Samuel ch.18 v.'s 6–15.

6. Early in his reign David was promised that his kingdom would last forever, though on his death-bed he told Solomon that the promise depended on obedience.

   The gospels of Matthew and Luke contain family-trees of Jesus and both claim Jesus was a descendant of David.

   a. Read Matthew ch.1 v.1 and Luke ch.3 v.31.

7. Why did David become so famous in Israel's history?

David's tomb, Jerusalem

Solomon

Solomon, David's son, built a temple and a palace in Jerusalem.

1. a. Read 2 Chronicles ch.3 v.'s 3–8.

   b. Name the three main rooms of the temple.

   c. The insides of the rooms were overlaid with, what?

The ruins of Zarethan: nearby was a bronze foundry where implements for the temple were made.

   d. Read 1 Kings ch.7 v.'s 1 and 2.

   e. Which was bigger, the temple or the palace?

Solomon also rebuilt cities, including Megiddo

Part of the ruins of Megiddo

He began a sea trade operating from the Gulf of Aqaba.

2. a. Find the Gulf of Aqaba on a map.
   b. Which sea is the Gulf a part of?
   c. Read 1 Kings ch.9 v.28 and 1 Kings ch.10 v.22.
   d. Where is "the land of Ophir"?
   e. State one precious metal and one type of animal his sailors brought back.

He developed a trade in horses and chariots.

3. a. Read 1 Kings ch.10 v.'s 28 and 29.
   b. How much more did a chariot cost than a horse?

The remains of one of Solomon's stables, and of a manger

Solomon was famous for his wealth and his wisdom.

4. a. Read 1 Kings ch.3 v.'s 4–14, 1 Kings ch.10 v.'s 14 and 15, and 1 Kings ch.4 v.'s 32–34.

His wisdom was tested.

    b. Read 1 Kings ch.3 v.'s 16–28.

    c. What would you have done if you had been the king?

He divided Israel into twelve districts, each providing one month's supply for the palace.

5. Read 1 Kings ch.4 v.'s 22 and 23 for one day's supply.

Perhaps Solomon overtaxed his subjects. When he died the people of northern Israel asked the new king, Rehoboam, to make their lives easier; he replied he would make their lives harder. So they rebelled and set up their own kingdom.

6. a. Read 1 Kings ch.12 v.'s 1–20.

    b. Rehoboam said his father beat the people with, what? He himself would beat them with, what?

7. 1 Kings ch.11 v.'s 1–13 gives another reason for the kingdom splitting. What is it?

Isaiah

For two hundred years the two kingdoms, Judah in the south, Israel in the north, existed independently. Then both were overwhelmed by the Assyrian empire.

1. Find Assyria on a map.

King Tiglath-Pileser (745–727) of Assyria in his war chariot.

King Sennacherib (705–681) of Assyria after his conquest of Lachish, in Judah.

One prophet who saw this event as God's punishment for sin was Isaiah.

2. a. Read Isaiah ch.1 and list FOUR sins God's people had committed.
   b. Read Isaiah ch.5 v.'s 1–7. What does he compare the vineyard to? State, briefly, what God is going to do with it.

The punishment will become cosmic.

3. a. Read Isaiah ch.13 v.'s 9, 10, 13 and ch.30 v.'s 27, 28, 30.
   b. What mood will the Lord be in?
   c. What disasters will occur in the sky and on earth? Draw a picture combining them.

Isaiah emphasised his message of calamity by walking about naked. Read Isaiah ch.20 v.'s 2–4.

But some people – those who repent and are righteous – will be saved. They will live in peace under the rule of a descendant of King David.

4. a. Read Isaiah ch.9 v.'s 2–7 and ch.11 v.'s 1–9.
   b. Imagine you are one of the survivors. Describe what you have been through, and how you will live now.

      Notice the people who are saved will include non-Jews, i.e gentiles.
   c. Read Isaiah ch.19 v.'s 24, 25 and ch.25 v.'s 6,7.

Another idea Isaiah raises is, there will be no more death, and some, at least, who have died will be brought back to life.

5. a. Read Isaiah ch.25 v.8 and ch.26. v.19.
   b. Who do you think is meant by "Those of our people" (ch.26 v.19)?

In the second half of the book, commonly thought to have been written by somebody else, there is a description of a servant who suffered for the sake of others.

6. a. Read Isaiah ch.52 v.13 – ch.53 v.12.
   b. Who do you think this figure came to be identified with?

Ezekiel

The Assyrian conquest was followed by the Babylonian conquest. The Jews rebelled and some of them were taken into exile in Babylonia (in 597, 587 and 582 B.C.).

A Babylonian inscription recording the capture of Jerusalem in 597, and the removal of Jews to Babylonia

Ezekiel, a priest, and one of the exiles, preached that the Jews had rebelled against the Lord. He mentions violence and idolatry in particular. The present sufferings are a punishment.

1. Read Ezekiel ch.7 v.'s 1–3, 15, 16.
2. He reinforced his message by signs:
    a. Read Ezekiel ch.4 v.'s 1–7.
    b. Read Ezekiel ch.5 v.'s 1–4.
    c. What do you think the thirds represent?
    d. Check your answers with Ezekiel ch.5 v.12.
    e. What would you say about the society you live in? What would you do to demonstrate your views?

The ruins of Babylon:

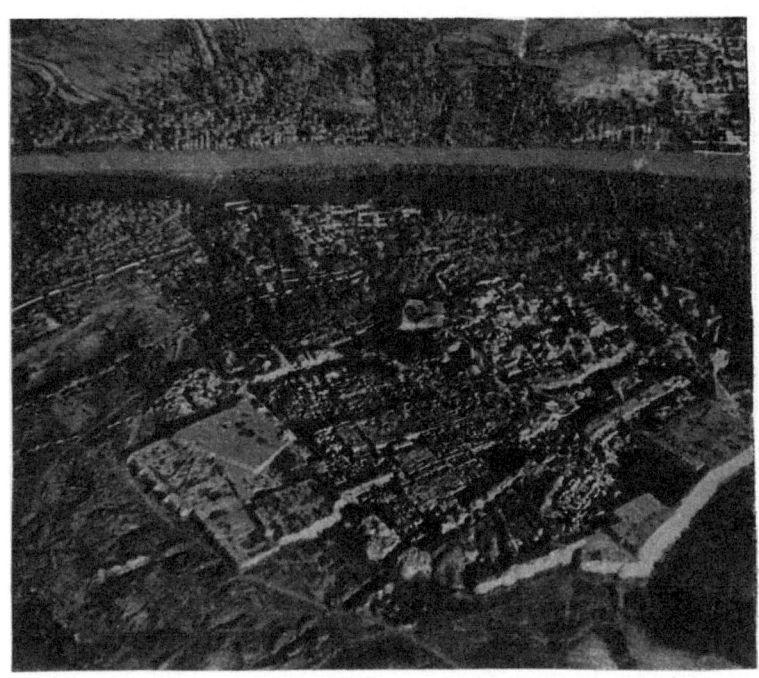

a. An aerial view

b. A close-up view

Amidst the punishment, good people will be spared and the land will be restored. A king like David will rule a united country, secure for ever.

3. a. Read Ezekiel ch.37 v.'s 1–10.

   b. What do you think the bones represent?

   c. Check your answer with v.11

   d. Read on, v.'s 12, 13 and 14. Is God going to bring the dead back to life or are the down-trodden people being compared to dead people?

Ezekiel taught:

4. Punishment will fall only on the sinner.

   a. Read Ezekiel ch.18 v.20. Compare Deuteronomy ch. 24 v.16.

   b. Do you remember King David's punishments for ensuring that Uriah was killed?

   c. Read Joshua ch.7.

5. If a sinner repents (regrets his sin) and acts properly, he will be forgiven.

   a. Read Ezekiel ch.18 v.'s 21–23.

   b. Make up a story about a repentant sinner.

   c. Read Luke ch.15 v.'s 11–32.

The Return

The Babylonian empire gave way to the Persian empire. The Persian king, Cyrus, commanded the re-building of the temple in Jerusalem, and encouraged the Jews in Babylonia to return home to work on it (538 B.C.).

1. a. Read Ezra ch.1 v.'s 2–4 and ch.6 v.'s 3–5.
   b. What, in these commands, shows Cyrus to be an unusually mild ruler?
   c. Refer to a map and work out how many kilometres there are, approximately, between Babylon and Jerusalem.
   Is it nearer 500 or 1,000 or 1,500?

The tomb of king Cyrus

The remains of the palace of the Persian king, Darius

A gateway showing King Darius on his throne being held up by his subjects

Following the rebellions, Jerusalem had been reduced to ruins.

2. a. Read 2 Kings ch.25 v.'s 8–10.

    b. Imagine you are one of the returning Jews and describe Jerusalem, and your feelings, when you first saw it.

People already living in and around Judah resented the newcomers and obstructed their work.

3. a. Read Ezra ch.4 v.'s 4,5 and Nehemiah ch.4 v.'s 1–3 and v.'s 7–9.

    b. State three ways in which the inhabitants tried to prevent the reconstructions.

Nonetheless, the temple was re-built (finished 515) and, much later, the city walls (437?).

The prophets Haggai and Zechariah looked forward to a golden age.

4. a. Read Haggai ch.2 v.'s 6–9 and Zechariah ch.8 v.'s 3, 7,8, 12.

    b. Consider some of the aims: conquests, prosperity, peace, justice, good harvests, faithfulness to and protection from God. Which of these would be part of your golden age?

    c. What would you yourself add?

Daniel

The Persians were replaced by the Greeks. In the C. 2nd one ruler tried to force the worship of the Greek god, Zeus, upon the Jews.

The book of Daniel shows the superiority of the Lord.

1. The Lord gives the ability to interpret dreams:

    a. Read Daniel ch.2 v.'s 26–28, 31–35.
    b. What do you think the statue represents?
    c. What do you think the stone represents?
    d. Check your answers by reading v.'s 36–45.

2. He judges rulers:

    a. Read Daniel ch.4.
    b. Why was King Nebuchadnezzar made to live like an animal?
    c. Read Daniel ch.5.
    d. Make a comic-strip account of "the writing on the wall". Divide a page into eight squares. Write headings for the squares as follows:

        1. Banquet. Sacred cups. Statues
        2. The writing
        3. Whoever interpreted it, be rewarded.
        4. Wise men not understand it.
        5. Queen mother suggested Daniel.
        6. Daniel stated Neb.'s and Bel.'s sins.
        7. He interpreted writing.
        8. That night!

        Draw pictures of each heading; include (where it helps) "bubble" speech, as in a comic.

3. He saves his followers:
   a. Read Daniel ch.3.
   b. Describe and explain any situation where you would refuse to obey a command, despite the threat of severe punishment.
   c. Read Daniel ch.6.

Darius the great

   d. Imagine you are Daniel. Describe your feelings when you were arrested and thrown to the lions. Write an account of your night in the pit.

Many people who are not saved from death will, even so, live again, eternally, some in happiness, some in unhappiness.

Daniel expected the new life to start about three and a half years after the misuse of the Temple, that is, about 163 BC.

4. a. Read Daniel ch.12.
   b. What would happen to Daniel himself?

Old Testament Crossword

Across

1. The number of books in the Bible (5,3)

3. One of the two sections of the Bible (3)

5. A monster (5)

7. The modern theory of life (9)

9. The first man (4)

11. She came from man (3)

13. The couple started it (3)

15. The number of days it rained during the flood (5)

17. It sounds like the Hebrew for "mixed up" (7)

19. The name means "Father of many" (7)

21. His new name which became that of the country (6)

23. The land which was to be "the promised land" (6)

25. Ten, in particular (12)

Down

2. God made them on the fourth day (5)

4. The first garden (4)

6. The tempter in the garden (5)

8. Where Goliath came from (4)

10. The number of people on Noah's ark (5)

12. The mountain where the ark grounded (6)

14. The sinful city of Genesis ch.19 (5)

16. Abraham and Sarah's son (5)

18. His father's favourite (6)

20. "Prime minister" of what new homeland? (5)

22. The four letters of God's name (4)

24. The plague that made Pharaoh let the people go (8)

26. The first conquest in "the promised land" (7)

27. One thing not to do (5)

28. He anointed Saul (6)

29. Samson was one (5)

30. The number of times Saul disobeyed (3)

31. It became the capital (9)

32. One country conquered by David (4)

33. One of Solomon's grand buildings (6)

34. The prophet who rebuked the king (6)

35. Something else Solomon was famous for (6)

36. A descendant of David (5)

37. Non-Jews (8)

38. One of the two kingdoms (5)

39. He compared Israel to a poor vineyard (6)

40. In a valley they came to life (5)

41. A prophet who was a priest (7)

42. The statue was struck by one (5)

43. The number of years until God's kingdom (5)

44. It will be no more (4)

45. Many will rise (4)

46. Eternal for some (4)

Answers to O.T. Crossword

Across	**Down**
1. Sixty-six	1. Stars
3. Old or New	4. Eden
5. Rahab	6. Snake
7. Evolution	8. Gath
9. Adam	10. Eight
11. Eve	12. Ararat
13. Sin	14. Sodom
15. Forty	16. Isaac
17. Babylon	18. Joseph
19. Abraham	20. Egypt
21. Israel	22. YHWH
23. Canaan	24. Passover
25. Commandments	26. Jericho
27. Steal	28. Samuel
29. Judge	30. Two
31. Jerusalem	32. Edom
33. Temple	34. Nathan
35. Wisdom	36. Jesus
37. Gentiles	38. Judah
39. Isaiah	40. Bones
41. Ezekiel	42. Stone
43. Three	44. Evil
45. Dead	46. Life

THE

NEW

TESTAMENT

The Gospels

The first four books of The New Testament, known as The Gospels, describe the life of Jesus, founder of Christianity.

1. What does the word "gospel" mean?
2. Which gospel states this meaning?
3. Name the authors of the gospels.
4. Which is the shortest gospel?
5. Which is the longest gospel?
6. Which are "The Synoptic Gospels"?
7. Why are they so-called?
8. Which gospel begins like a letter?
9. Which gospel starts with Jesus' family tree?
10. Which gospel writer seems to have written also "The Acts of the Apostles"?
11. Which gospel has different endings?
12. Which gospel concludes by saying Jesus did "many other things"?

The first page of Mark's Gospel in the Lindisfarne Gospels (c. 700)

The first page of John's Gospel in William Tyndale's New Testament (1535)

The Nativity

The gospels of Matthew and Luke describe the nativity of Jesus.

1. a. What does the word 'nativity' mean?
   b. Do the gospels of Mark and John begin with Jesus as a baby, a child or a man?
2. a. Read Matthew ch.1 v.18 – ch.2 v.23 and Luke ch.1 v.'s 26–38 and ch.2 v.'s 1–20, 39, 40.
   b. Fill in the colunns:

	Matt.	Lk.
Who did the angel appear to?		
In what town did the angel appear?		
Why were Joseph and Mary in Bethlehem?		
Who visited the baby Jesus?		
In what town did Jesus grow up?		

The traditional site where the angel Gabriel appeared to Mary,
now part of the Church of the Annunciation, Nazareth

The traditional site of the birth of Jesus,
now part of the Church of the Nativity, Bethlehem

3. When was Jesus born? Traditionally, at the start of the Christian calendar, and so the years before are known as B.C. (Before Christ). But,

   a. Herod the Great was king of Judaea when Jesus was born, and Herod died in 4 B.C.

   b. There may have been "a census" (Luke ch.2 v.1) in 8 B.C.

   c. The "star" (Matthew ch.2 v.2) <u>may</u> have been an unusual formation of the planets Jupiter, Saturn and Venus which occurred early in 7 B.C.

4. What are frankincense and myrrh? What are they commonly used for?

Frankincense

Myrrh

5. Write a play combining the visits of the wise men and the shepherds to Jesus. Remember, for your speech, that the wise men would have been educated; the shepherds, probably not.

Childhood, Baptism and Temptations

The Gospels contain only one story of Jesus as a boy.

1. a. Read Luke ch.2 v.'s 41–52.
   b. How would you feel if someone in your class caused amazement by his/her "intelligent answers" (Luke ch.2 v.47)?
   c. What do you think of Jesus, firstly, staying without his parents knowing and, secondly, of his reply when his mother asked him why he had done it?

**The site of the temple, Jerusalem.
The mosque, in the middle of it, dates from the C.7th**

When Jesus was about thirty years old, he was baptized by a prophet known as John the Baptist.

2. What is baptism and why is water a part of it ?
3. a. Read Mark ch.1 v.'s 1–11.
   b. What was John's purpose in God's plan?
   c. State <u>two</u> things John said about the man who would come after him.
   d. State two things which happened when Jesus came out of the water.

The river Jordan at Bethabara, the traditional place of Jesus's baptism.

"Then the spirit led Jesus into the desert to be tempted by the Devil" (Matthew ch.4 v.1)

4. a. Read Matthew ch.4 v.'s 1–11.

   b. Consider each of the temptations. Why do you think the Devil chose it in particular?

The Mount of Temptation, the traditional location of Jesus' temptations. Notice the monastery on the side of the mountain.

Jesus began his ministry.

A C1ˢᵗ picture of Jesus, the earliest one known.

The Disciples

1. What does the word "disciple" mean?

2. a. Read Mark ch.3 v.'s 16–19.
   b. Write down the names of the twelve disciples.

3. a. Read Luke ch.6 v.'s 14–16.
   b. Which disciple listed by Mark is not listed by Luke?
   c. Who does Luke name instead?

4. a. What does the name "Peter" mean?
   b. Read Matthew ch.16 v.'s 13–20.
   c. Why did Jesus call Simon "Peter"?

C.3rd picture of an apostle, commonly identified as Simon Peter

5. Who was Peter's brother?

Ruins of Capernaum, including those of a synagogue (far right) and of a church (far left) built over a house which may have been Peter's (read Mark ch.1 v.'s 21, 29–31).

6. a. Which other two disciples were brothers?
   b. What nickname did Jesus give them?
   c. Read Luke ch.9 v.'s 51–56 for an incident where they lived up to this nickname.

7. What was the profession of both pairs of brothers? Read about their call to become disciples.

8. a. Read Matthew ch.9 v.'s 9–13.
   b. What was Matthew's profession?

9. Which two disciples are mentioned in the feeding of the 5,000?

10. Which disciple betrayed Jesus?

11. a. Read John ch.20 v.'s 24–29.
    b. Why is Thomas known as "doubting"?

12. Which of the Gospel writers may also have been disciples?

The tree, according to tradition, from which Judas hanged himself.

Teachings

A synagogue in Nazareth, perhaps built on the site of one used by Jesus

1. a. What is a synagogue?

   b. Read Mark ch.6 v.'s 1, 2.

Jesus said that he had not "come to do away with the law of Moses and the teachings of the prophets ... but to make their teachings come true" (Matthew ch.5 v.17).

2. a. What, according to Jesus, are the two most important commandments of all? Read Mark ch.12 v.'s 29–31, and compare these verses with Deuteronomy ch.6 v's 4, 5 and Leviticus ch.19 v.18.

   b. "Love the Lord": Read "The Lord's prayer" Matthew ch.6 v.'s 9–13. The traditional form of this prayer is:

"Our Father who art in heaven, hallowed be thy name. Thy kingdom come, Thy will be done, on earth as it is in heaven. Give us this day our daily bread; and forgive us our trespasses, as we forgive those who trespass against us; and lead us not into temptation, but deliver us from evil. For thine is the kingdom, the power and the glory, for ever and ever. Amen."

Which form of the prayer do you prefer?

The cloister of the church of Our father, Jerusalem

    c. "Love your neighbour." Read "The parable of the good Samaritan", Luke ch.10 v.'s 30–37.

    d. What is a parable?

    e. Make up a modern-day version of "The good Samaritan".

Everyone should try to obey the commandments; if they disobey (sin) and are truly sorry (repent), they will be forgiven.

3. a. Read the parables of "The lost", Luke ch. 15.

    b. If you had been the elder brother, would you have acted in the same way?

    c. Is it fair that "…there will be more joy in heaven over one sinner who repents than over ninety- nine respectable people who do not need to repent" (Luke ch.15 v.7)?

There will be a day of judgement.

4. a. Read Matthew ch.25 v.'s 31–33 for a vivid description of separating the good from the bad.

b. Compare this account with Matthew ch.24 v.'s 30, 31. Is there any basic difference?

c. Compare Matthew ch.24 v.31 with Matthew ch.13 v.41. Is there any basic difference?

Matthew ch. 25 ends with, the unrighteous "…will be sent off to eternal punishment, but the righteous will go to eternal life" (v.46) – life in heaven, bliss with God e.g. Matthew ch.13 v.43, and punishment in hell, torment by fire e.g. Matthew ch.13 v.42.

At least some who have died will be brought back to life. When Jesus is asked about the resurrection he implies that only good people will be raised from death.

5. a. Read Matthew ch.22 v.30, Mark ch.12 v.25, Luke ch.20 v.'s 34–36. Compare Luke ch.14 v.14. But read also, Matthew ch.10 v. 28 and John ch.5 v.'s 28, 29.

b. Would it be fair if bad people who are alive on the day of judgement are punished whilst bad people who are dead are not?

c. Read the parable of "The rich man and Lazarus" (Luke ch.16 v.'s 19–31). What problem does this raise for the day of judgement?

Jesus taught that he had a special relationship with God. He implied that he was the son of God, even God himself.

6. a. Find out the meanings of the Trinity and of the Incarnation.

b. Read "The Transfiguration" (Mark ch.9 v.'s 2–8). What does the voice call Jesus?

c. What does transfiguration mean?

d. Imagine you were one of the disciples present at this event. What would it have meant to you?

Jesus also implied that he was the Messiah, the king, a descendant of king David who would rule a glorious Israel.

7. a. Remember Matthew ch.16 v.'s 13–20.

b. Read John ch.4 v.'s 25, 26.

c. Read the note "The Messiah".

"Messiah" is a Hebrew word; in Greek it is translated as "Christos", and in English as "Christ". So Jesus is commonly called Jesus Christ; his believers, Christians, and his teachings, Christianity.

The interior of the church of the Transfiguration on Mt. Tabor

Mt. Tabor

Miracles

The word comes from the Latin 'miraculum' meaning 'a wonderful thing'.

1. How would you describe a miracle?

   Jesus "...healed many people, and all those who were ill kept pushing their way to him..." (Mark ch.3 v.10).

2. Look through Mark's gospel and find an example of Jesus healing:

   a. A paralysed person.

   b. An insane person.

   c. A blind person.

Throughout the ages there have been claims of miracles. A well-known 'healer' of the C.20th was Harry Edwards. The following is an extract from an interview given by Mr Edwards in 1964:

"I had 8,750 letters this week. The majority who write to me have been told they are incurable. As a result of my meditations 80 per cent record a measure of improvement. 30 per cent of these have a complete recovery."

3. Find out why Lourdes, a town in southern France, is associated with miracles

Bernadette and her home.

Bernadette and her home

The site of the 'appearance' and sick people hoping to be cured.

Three occasions are recorded of Jesus bringing someone back to life.

4. a. Read 'the raising of Lazarus' (John ch.11 v.'s 1–44).

b. Write a play, featuring Jesus, Martha, Mary and the crowd, from the time of Jesus arriving at Bethany to Lazarus coming out of the tomb (v.'s 17–44).

Some people have 'died', been resuscitated and declared that whilst 'dead' they experienced an after-life: commonly, they heard themselves pronounced 'dead', viewed their own body, realised they had a new sort of body, moved quickly through a tunnel, met relatives who had died, met a being who prompted them to consider their life, reached a barrier, but returned to their earthly body.

5. What would you think if a person who had 'died', and was brought back to life, knew what was said and done by those around them after he/she had 'died', and this was confirmed by those concerned?

Not all of Jesus' miracles were of healing, nor on people; some concerned water, food, fish, pigs, even a tree! These are known as 'nature miracles'. One of the most famous is 'the feeding of the 5,000'.

6. a. Read John ch.6 v.'s 1–13.

   b. Imagine you were the boy, and describe the event.

The church of the Multiplication of the Loaves and Fishes

The interior of the church of the multiplication.

Part of the floor of the church of the multiplication

7. What one miracle would you like to see happen today?

The Closing Stages

During his ministry Jesus fell out with the religious leaders – by his teaching about himself, by his interpretations of some of the law and probably by his accusation that they were hypocrites. Their hostility may have been made worse by his power and popularity. They feared the Romans might see his influence as a threat and act against the nation.

1. Read, for example, Luke ch.6 v.'s 1–5; John ch.5 v.'s 15–18; Mark ch.7 v.'s 1, 2, 5, 15; Matthew ch.23 v.'s 27, 28; Mark ch.3 v.22; Luke ch.20 v.19; John ch.11 v.'s 47, 48.

Figures of a Priest and a High Priest

Judas Iscariot, one of the disciples, offered to help the leaders arrest him.

2. a. Read Matthew ch.26 v.'s 14–16.

The denarius, a silver coin. How many were given to Judas?

b. Can you think of any reasons, apart from money, for Judas being willing to betray Jesus?

The Last Supper,
the Arrest and the Trial before the High Priest

The last meal Jesus and his disciples ate together is known as "the last supper".

Room of the "Last Supper", Jerusalem

During the meal Jesus took bread and a cup of wine.

1. a. Read Matthew ch.26 v.'s 26–28.

   b. When Jesus speaks of his blood being "poured out for many for the forgiveness of sins" (v.28), he is implying that he is a, what?

   c. How, by comparing his body to the bread and his blood to the wine could Jesus also be teaching togetherness, and life, and eternal life? See John ch.6 v.'s 48–51, 40

Afterwards the twelve went to Gethsemane, a place on the Mount of Olives.

Steps probably used on the way to the Mount of Olives

They were there when Judas Iscariot led a group, sent by the religious leaders, to arrest Jesus.

2. a. Read Matthew ch.26 v.'s 36–56.

   b. What words in v.'s 36–46 show both Jesus's dread and bravery?

   c. Was Judas needed? Could the religious leaders have used a spy to watch Jesus's movements?

   d. Read the note "Judas Iscariot".

Jesus was taken to the High Priest

3. a. Read Matthew ch.26 v.'s 57–67.

The site of the trial, now covered by a church

b. Find out the meaning of "the Sanhedrin".

c. What verse in the passage shows that this was not a fair trial?

Nonetheless, the court decided that Jesus condemned himself by his reply to the High Priest.

d. What does "blasphemy" mean? Was Jesus guilty of it?

A pit in which Jesus may have been imprisoned after his condemnation

The Trial before Pilate, the Crucifixion and the Burial

Jesus was taken to Pilate.

1. a. Who was Pilate? Read Matthew ch.27 v.2.
   b. Using reference material, find out more about him.
   c. What <u>one</u> question did Pilate ask Jesus in all four gospels?
   d. Why was this question important?
   e. According to Matthew's or Mark's gospel, what did Pilate see as the real reason for Jesus' arrest?
   f. Why did he himself condemn Jesus?

The traditional site where Pilate sentenced Jesus to be crucified.

2. a. Read Psalm 22 and Mark ch.15 v.'s 22–37.
   b. Find details in the readings which are similar.
   c. How do you explain these similarities?

**The traditional site of the crucifixion,
now covered by the Church of the Holy Sepulchre**

3. a. Read John ch.19 v.'s 38–42.
   b. What reason is suggested for Joseph of Arimathea burying Jesus?
   c. What do we learn about Jewish burial customs?

**The traditional site of the tomb of Jesus,
within the Church of the Holy Sepulchre**

An alternative site, known as the garden tomb, of Jesus' burial

The Resurrection

1. a. Read Matthew ch.28 v.'s 1–10; Mark ch.16 v.'s 1–8; Luke ch.24 v.'s 1–12; John ch.20v.'s 1–18.

   b. Are the following statements true or false for <u>all</u> four gospels?

   (i) At least one woman went to the tomb.

   (ii) She / they went there early Sunday morning.

   (iii) The stone was moved.

   (iv) Jesus had gone.

   (v) There were guards.

   (vi) There was at least one angel.

   (vii) Someone at the tomb spoke to the woman/women.

   (viii) She / they met Jesus.

   (ix) She / they told the disciples what had happened.

   (x) At least one disciple went to the tomb.

A tomb showing part of the stone used to seal the entrance

2. Consider carefully the following questions:

   a. How could Jesus have come back to life?

   b. If the disciples took his body, would they have gone on to preach his message – including the resurrection – so fearlessly, risking torture and death?
   Read Acts ch.4 v.'s 1–22; Acts ch.5 v.'s 27–42;
   Romans ch.8 v.'s 35–39.

   c. If somebody else took his body, why?

   d. How did the disciples who, Luke says, were at first disbelieving, come to believe so definitely that Jesus had been raised from the dead? This belief was fundamental. Read 1 Corinthians ch.15 v.'s 12–19.

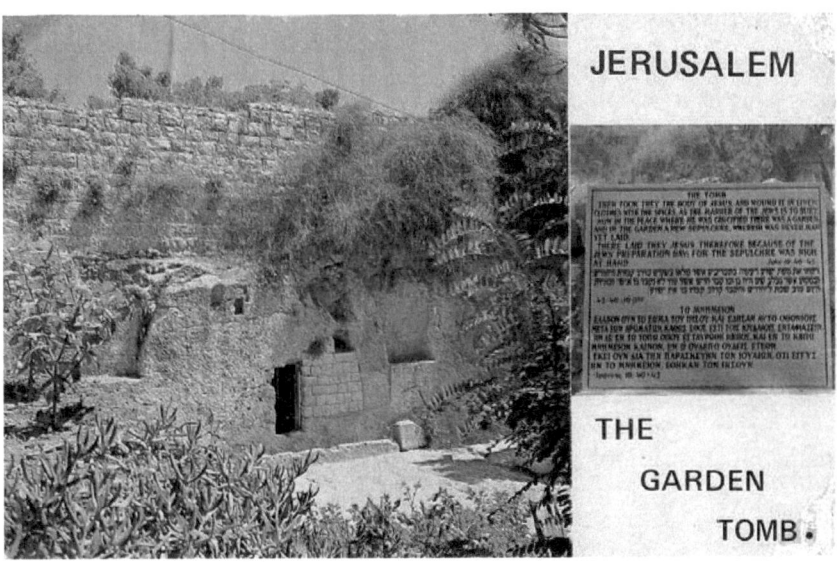

JERUSALEM

THE GARDEN TOMB.

Post-resurrection Appearances and the Ascension

Following his resurrection, Jesus appeared to his disciples on various occasions – one famous appearance was to "Doubting Thomas".

1. a. Read John ch.20 v.'s 24–29.

   b. Make a comic-strip account of "Doubting Thomas"; for example, divide a page into four squares; write headings for the squares as follows:

      (i) Thomas disbelieves.

      (ii) A week later. The disciples together.

      (iii) Jesus appears. Offers proof to Thomas.

      (iv) Thomas believes. Jesus rebukes.

      Draw pictures of each heading; include – where it helps – 'bubble' speech, as in a comic.

2. Would <u>you</u> believe without seeing? Discuss. Are there any occasions where you believe without seeing?

3. Jesus suggested he wanted Peter to lead his followers.

   a. Read John ch.21 v.'s 15–17

4. Finally, 40 days after his resurrection, Jesus ascended to heaven.

   a. Read Acts ch.1 v.'s 6–14.

   b. Imagine you were one of the disciples watching Jesus go and, considering the past, and the future, describe your thoughts and feelings.

The traditional site of Peter's appointment

Traditionally, Jesus' footprint made during his ascension.

The Early Church

The Book of Acts describes the beginnings of the Christian church – the acts of the apostles.

1. a. What is the difference between 'disciples' and 'apostles'?

   b. Why do you think the name changed?

Jesus promised his disciples that they would be filled with power, the power of the Holy Spirit.

2. a. Read Acts ch.2 v.'s 1–13.

   b. Find out the meaning of the word 'Pentecost'.

   c. Think imaginatively of ways in which 'wind' and 'fire' fitted this occasion, e.g wind 'blew away', fire 'burnt up', their fears.

   d. What particular power or ability was given immediately? How would this help the apostles' work?

The apostles preached plainly and boldly, and performed miracles. More and more people believed. The religious leaders tried to silence them – they were threatened and punished. Stephen became the first Christian martyr.

"They seized Stephen and took him before the Council" (Acts ch.6 v.12b).

3. a. Read Acts ch.7 v.'s 51–60.

   b. Compare v.'s 51–53 with Mark ch.12 v.'s 1–12. Who do you think is meant by (i) the tenants? (ii) the slaves? (iii) the son?

   c. Which verses between v.'s 54–60 are similar to Luke ch.22 v.69, Luke ch.23 v.34 and Luke ch.23 v.46?

   d. Who, so it seems, wrote the Book of Acts? Compare Acts ch.1 v.1 with Luke ch.1 v.'s 1–4.

Stephen's gate, Jerusalem

The traditional site where Stephen was stoned

One person who persecuted the church was a young man named Saul. But,

4. a. Read Acts ch.9 v.'s 1–9.

   b. For another account of a sudden, religious experience read this passage:

   "I was in perfect health: we were on our sixth day of tramping, and in good training... I felt neither fatigue, hunger, nor thirst, and my state of mind was equally healthy... I was subject to no anxiety, either near or remote, for we had a good guide, and there was not a shadow of uncertainty about the road we should follow. I can best describe the condition in which I was by calling it a state of equilibrium. When all at once I experienced a feeling of being raised above myself, I felt the presence of God – I tell of the thing just as I was conscious of it – as if his goodness and his power were penetrating me altogether. The throb of emotion was so violent that I could barely tell the boys to pass on and not wait for me. I then sat down on a stone, unable to stand any longer, and my eyes overflowed with tears. I thanked God that in the course of my life he had taught me to know him, that he sustained my life and took pity both on the insignificant creature and on the sinner that I was. I begged him ardently that my life might be consecrated to the doing of his will. I felt his reply, which was that I should do his will from day to day, in humility and poverty, leaving him, the Almighty God, to be judge of whether I should some time be called to bear witness more conspicuously. Then, slowly, the ecstasy left my heart; that is, I felt that God had withdrawn the communion which he had granted, and I was able to walk on, but very slowly, so strongly was I still possessed by the interior emotion." (from "The Varieties of Religious Experience," quoted by William James).

   c. Do you think <u>you</u> could become a believer in this way?

Peter realised that gentiles (non-Jews) as well as Jews could join the church.

5. a. Read Acts ch.10. What was the connection between Cornelius and Peter's vision?

The house, according to tradition, of Simon the tanner (Acts ch.10 v.6)

   b. Read Acts ch.15 v.'s 1–29. What were the particular rules for gentiles who became Christians?

Saul, who became better known as Paul, undertook missionary journeys in countries around the Mediterranean sea.

6. a. The following cities are some where he preached; using an atlas, find them and mark them on the outline map provided: Antioch, Paphos, Lystra, Philippi, Thessalonica, Athens, Corinth, Ephesus and Troas.

   b. Read Acts ch.17 v.'s 16–34. In no more than 100 words describe what happened when Paul was at Athens.

Finally, Paul was arrested and taken to Rome to be tried by the Emperor. The Book of Acts ends with him there.

7. a. Mark Rome on the map.

   b. Find out what might have become of him.

An altar "To the unknown God"

C.1st pictures of Peter (left) and Paul

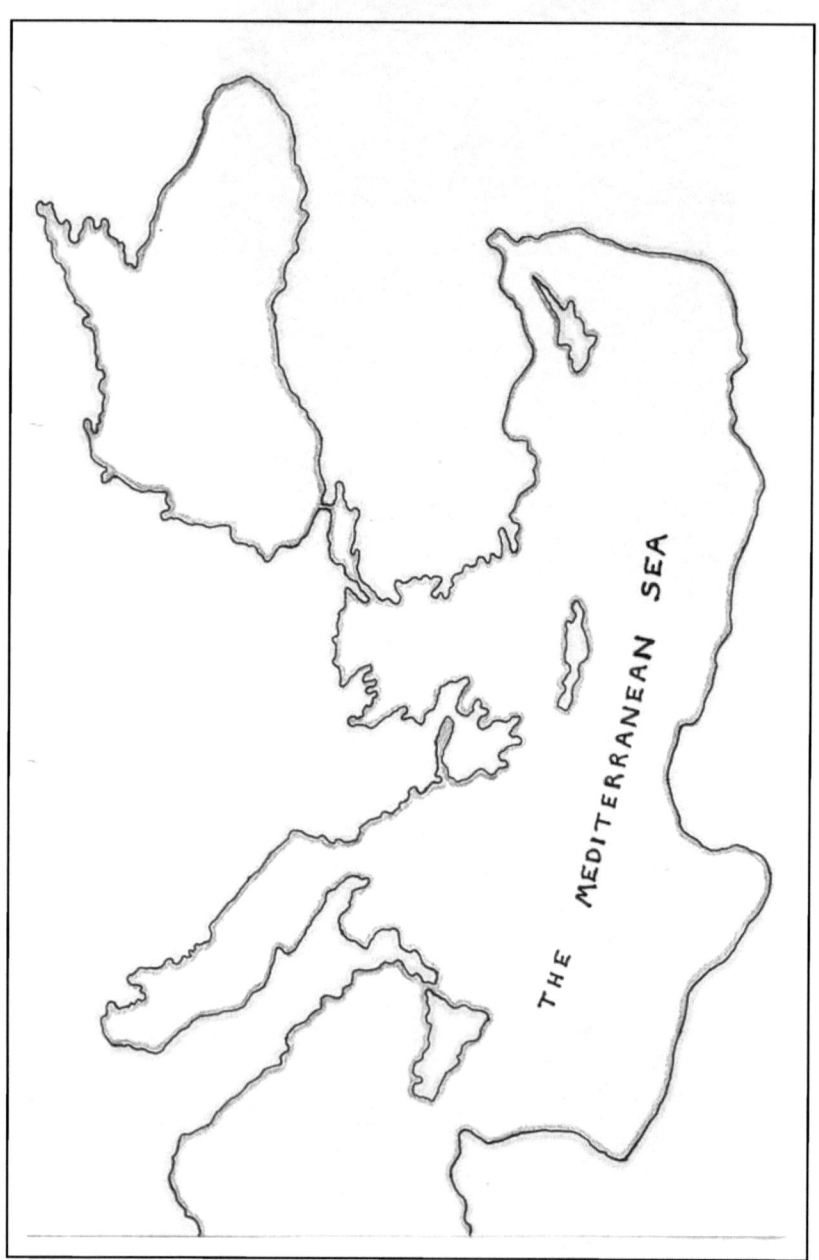

The Letters

As Christianity spread, letters were written to churches and individuals, and some are included in The New Testament.

1. a. How many?
   b. How many were written by Paul?
   c. Find out their old name.

A part of Paul's letter to the Romans, dating from the C.3rd.

Paul taught "justification ('making right') by faith."

2. a. What does it mean? Read Romans ch.3 v.'s 20–26, 28.

   But believers must not disregard the law.

   b. Read Romans ch.3 v.31, ch.6 v.15; 2 Corinthians ch.5 v.10; Ephesians ch.5 v.5.

At times there is the notion that God decides in advance what will happen in a person's life. This is called predestination.

3. a. Read Galatians ch.1 v.15.
   b. Is predestination fair?
      Consider Paul's answer in Romans ch.9 v.'s 18–23.

The writers expected the day of judgement to be soon.

4. a. Read 1 Thessalonians ch.4 v.'s 15–17.
   b. What other features about the day are mentioned in 2Thessalonians ch.1 v.'s 6–10, ch.2 v.8 and 2 Peter ch.3 v.'s 10–13.

An early picture of Jesus giving Peter and Paul "crowns of righteousness".

5. What did the writers have to say about:

    a. Rulers? Read Romans ch.13 v.'s 1, 2, 6, 7; 1 Peter ch.2 v.'s 13, 14.

    b. Slaves / masters? Read Ephesians ch.6 v.' s 5–9; Colossians ch.4 v.1; 1 Peter ch.2 v.18.

    c. Wives / husbands? Read Ephesians ch.5 v.'s 22–25, 33; Titus ch.2 v.'s 4,5; 1Peter ch.3 v.7.

    d. Children / parents? Read Ephesians ch.6 v.'s 1–4; Colossians ch.3 v.'s 20, 21.

6. Discuss the following statements:

    a. "What does a believer have in common with an unbeliever?" (2 Corinthians ch.6 v. 15).

    b. "A person will reap exactly what he sows." (Galatians ch. 6 v.7).

    c. "…the love of money is a source of all kinds of evil." (1 Timothy ch.6 v.10).

    d. "What did we bring into the world? Nothing! What can we take out of the world? Nothing!" (1 Timothy ch.6 v.7).

7. a. Read 1 Corinthians ch.13.

   b. Do you consider it to be a good piece of writing? Explain your opinion.

8. Imagine you are a Christian leader today and write a letter to one of your churches advising its members what to concentrate upon, in their teachings, actions and policies. Pretend you know this particular church and comment, with approval or disapproval, on what is happening there.

Revelation

1. Who was the revelation to? Read the full title.

There is a vision of God in heaven.

2. a. Read Revelation ch.4.

   b. What were "the creatures" surrounding the throne? Each creature has come to be associated with a gospel writer. Try to find out which creature is linked with which writer.

   Most of the visions, however, are of punishments.

3. a. Read, for example, Revelation ch.16.

The remains of Megiddo, northern Israel. "Hill of Megiddo" is the usual interpretation of Armageddon (Revelation ch.16 v.16).

3. b. Remind yourself of "The Passover." Look at the plagues listed in Exodus ch.'s 7, 8, 9 and 10. How many are similar to those listed in Revelation ch.16?

Yet bad people do not repent.

4. a. Read, for example, Revelation ch.9 v.'s 20, 21; ch.16 v. 9.

Good people wait.

   b. Read Revelation ch.6 v.'s 9–11.

**A coin showing the emperor Nero who persecuted Christians.
He is thought to be "the beast" referred to in Revelation ch.13 v.18**

   c. Do you know of anyone who has stood up for some belief – perhaps in defence of somebody – and suffered because of it?

Eventually, the devil will be thrown into a fire. The dead will be judged. Anyone whose name is not in "the book of the living" (Revelation ch.20 v.15) will also be condemned to the fire.

Judgement day as depicted by the C.16th artist, Pieter Bruegel the elder.

A new Jerusalem, the home of the righteous, will descend from heaven.

5. a. Read Revelation ch.21 v.'s 10–21.

   b. Draw a diagram – birds-eye view – of the new city, showing its shape, size and gates.

   c. What is it made of?

God and Jesus will live in "the Holy City" (Revelation ch.21 v.2) and reign "for ever and ever" (Revelation ch.22 v.5).

"…Now God's home is with mankind! He will live with them, and they shall be his people… He will wipe away all tears from their eyes. There will be no more death, no more grief or crying or pain. The old things have disappeared." (Revelation ch.21 v.'s 3, 4)

A new creation!

New Testament Crossword

Clues

Across

1. The place for the good (6)
2. The great day (3,2,9)
4. Last forever (7)
6. Peter's first name (5)
8. The Jewish leaders often set one for Jesus (4)
10. A way of describing sinners (4)
12. We should pay these demands (5)
14. A title for a king (9)
16. The first word of the two most important commandments (4)
18. It was left lying in the tomb (5)
20. One of the gifts given to the baby Jesus (5)
22. The Roman governor who sentenced Jesus (6)
24. Paul often travelled on one (4)
26. Made from olives (3)
28. Jesus brought him back to life (7)
30. Stories with meanings (8)
32. One was used to defend Jesus (5)
34. Jesus compared it to his body (5)

Down

1. The place for the bad (4)
3. One of the sins (4)
5. Where Jesus grew up (8)
7. The deeds of the apostles (4)
9. Jesus' earthly father (6)
11. The evil one (5)
13. The old name for the letters (8)
15. The dark time when Jesus was arrested (5)
17. A famous expression – overturned by Jesus – "an eye for an eye, and a…" (5)
19. A place famous for C.20th miracles (7)
21. The Hebrew word for Christ (7)
23. Where the boy Jesus was found (6)
24. Paul's name, at first (4)
25. The town which Joseph who buried Jesus came from (9)
27. The name of the mountain where Jesus was arrested (6)
29. Despite the large catch, it was not broken (3)
31. They visited the baby Jesus (9)
33. It means "good news" (6)

36. The most famous number of thousands Jesus fed (4)

35. Not only the person next door is one (9)

38. The river in which Jesus was baptized (6)

37. He doubted that Jesus had come back to life (6)

40. One came to Mary (5)

39. The betrayer – the crowd (3)

42. The name of the last meal Jesus ate with his disciples (3,4,6)

41. Jesus shed more than one at Lazarus's tomb (4)

44. "A person will – exactly what he

sows" (4)

43. The first name of a C20th healer (5)

46. Where Paul was living at the end

of the book of Acts (4)

45. The number of coins paid to the betrayer (6)

48. Jesus' "surname" (6)

47. The first name of Jesus' betrayer
(5)

50. John saw it descend from heaven
(3,3,9)

49. Where Paul debated with Greek teachers (6)

52. It means raising the dead to life (12)

51. The Jewish court found Jesus guilty of it (9)

54. The name for God, Son and Holy Spirit (7)

53. What the cautious servant did with his money (3)

55. The second word of the Lord's Prayer (6)

57. How Jesus was hit when the Sanhedrin condemned him (4)

Answers

Across	Down
1. Heaven	1. Hell
2. Day of Judgement	3. Envy
4. Eternal	5. Nazareth
6. Simon	7. Acts
8. Trap	9. Joseph
10. Lost	11. Devil
12. Taxes	13. Epistles
14. Sovereign	15. Night
16. Love	17. Tooth
18. Linen	19. Lourdes
20. Myrrh	21. Messiah
22. Pilate	23. Temple
24. Ship	24. Saul
26. Oil	25. Arimathea
28. Lazarus	27. Olives
30. Parables	29. Net
32. Sword	31. Shepherds
34. Bread	33. Gospel
36. Five	35. Neighbour
38. Jordan	37. Thomas
40. Angel	39. Led
42. The Last Supper	41. Tear
44. Reap	43. Harry
46. Rome	45. Thirty
48. Christ	47. Judas
50. The new Jerusalem	49. Athens
52. Resurrection	51. Blasphemy
54. Trinity	53. Hid
	55. Father
	57. Slap

NOTES

Taxation

There were:

1. Religious taxes, e.g.
   a. To the Temple (½ a shekel).
   b. To the priests (1%) (the 'first-fruits' of the land).
   c. On special occasions, e.g. the first-born child (5 shekels).

2. Roman taxes, e.g.
   a. On income and property (compare Income tax and The Community Charge).
   b. On sales and purchases (compare Value Added Tax).
   c. Customs duties.
   d. Road tolls.

The right to collect most of the Roman taxes was auctioned (i.e. sold to the highest bidder). The buyer used local people to be the collectors, and they made their money by collecting more than the tax itself.

Tax collectors were seen as sinners because they:

   a. Demanded more than the strict amount.

(Some tax collectors… asked him, "Teacher, what are we to do?"
"Don't collect more than is legal," he (John the Baptist) told them, Luke ch.3. Zacchaeus (a chief tax collector) … said to the Lord, "…if I have cheated anyone, I will pay him back four times as much." Luke ch.19 v.8. "Such people had a bad reputation everywhere at the time for their dishonesty and petty extortion." D.E. Nineham).

   b. Worked for the Romans – a hated, occupying force.
   c. Mixed with gentiles (unclean).
   d. Handled Roman coins. On the coins were engravings of Caesar's head, which could offend commandment 2 ('Do not make for yourselves images of anything…'), especially since the caesars were treated like gods.

The Sanhedrin

The Jewish Supreme Council.

Consisted of about 70 members (based on Moses' 70 helpers, Numbers ch.11, v.'s16, 17) – priests (High Priest the President), elders and scribes. Possessed some governing powers. Interpreted the law. Had right and left-wing parties. At first, mostly Sadducees, but, under Herod, more Pharisees.

Met in the Temple area. When sitting as a court, verdict reached by majority decision (though whereas for not guilty a majority, for guilty a ⅔ majority). Could not impose capital punishment (John ch.18 v.31).

The Pharisees

Religious sect. Began in C.2nd B.C. Pharisees generally from ordinary backgrounds. Main influence in the synagogues. Seems, popular.

Beliefs:
1. Law in all of O.T. and tradition.
2. Resurrection and judgement (rewards/punishments).
3. Coming Messianic kingdom.

The Sadducees

Religious sect. Began in C.2nd B.C. Sadducees generally from distinguished backgrounds. Main influence in the Temple. Seems, unpopular.

Beliefs:
1. Law only in the Pentateuch.
2. No resurrection. / judgement / rewards / punishments (Mark ch.12 v.18).
3. No coming Messianic kingdom.

The Scribes

Not just copyists. They interpreted the Law, applying it to daily situations and teaching it to pupils. Called "teachers of the Law".

Worked mainly in Jerusalem, in the Temple. Unpaid.

Not a religious or political party, but the scribes might have formed guilds (societies) (See 1 Chronicles ch.2 v.55).

Most belonged to the Pharisees.

Judas Iscariot

Iscariot – means, perhaps, 'a man of Kerioth' which may refer to a place in Judah.

Son of Simon.

One of the 12 disciples (mentioned last in the lists of the 12).

Jesus said that one of his disciples was "a devil" (John ch.6 v.70) and, according to John, Jesus meant Judas (John ch.6 v.71).

When Jesus was anointed, John says it was Judas who protested, why wasn't the ointment sold and the money given to the poor? John adds that Judas didn't really care about the poor. He carried the money bag and stole from it.

Went to the priests. Offered to betray Jesus. Paid 30 denarii.

During the last supper, Jesus said that one of his disciples would betray him. According to John he showed that it would be Judas. Judas then left the meal.

Led the soldiers to arrest Jesus in the Garden of Gethsemane. Identified Jesus with a kiss.

According to Matthew, repented, threw back the money and hanged himself. The money was used to buy a field, known as "Field of Blood" (Akeldama) because it as bought with "blood money".

According to Acts, Judas himself bought a field with the money. He had – it seems – a fatal accident in it and since he spilt his blood there, the field was known as "Field of Blood".

Disciples chose a replacement.

Was he:

1. A rogue? Did he himself decide to betray Jesus? If so, why?
    a. Greed (compare John ch.12 v.6).
    b. Disappointment that Jesus was not the kind of Messiah – a conqueror – that he had expected.
    c. An attempt to force Jesus to be the kind of Messiah he had expected by placing him in danger.
    d. Believing that Jesus was doomed, he betrayed him to escape punishment himself.
    e. Anger, perhaps because Jesus had rebuked him at the Anointing (John ch.12 v.'s 1–8).

2. A 'robot'? In the sense that he was,

   a. An instrument of God, compelled to fulfil the Scriptures, e.g. "…the scripture must come true that says, 'The man who shared my food turned against me'." (John ch.13 v.18. Compare Psalm 41 v.9, 'Even my best friend, the one I trusted most, the one who shared my food, has turned against me.').
   See, also, John ch.17 v.12; Acts ch.1 v.16.

   Compare Acts ch.1 v.20 (Psalm 69 v.25; 109 v.8).

   Compare Matthew ch.26 v.24; Mark ch.14 v.21.

   Compare Acts ch.1 v.25.

   b. An instrument of Satan, e.g. "Then Satan entered Judas…" (Luke ch.22 v.3) See, also, John ch.13 v.'s 2, 27.

3. As much a mixture of God's fore-knowledge, his own free-will and Satan's temptation as anyone else?

What did Judas betray? Where – and when – Jesus might be arrested without a great deal of commotion. The priests wanted to arrest Jesus "secretly" (Mark ch.14 v.1). They were afraid of a riot (e.g. Mark ch.14 v.2). Night-time, outside the city and out of doors presented a good chance of success.

They could have used a spy to watch Jesus' movements. But,

   a. Judas offered.

   b. He probably had 'inside information' (e.g. knew Jesus was going to Gethsemane after the Last Supper. N.B. John ch.18 v.2).

   c. He could easily – and quickly – identify Jesus (the crowd with Judas don't seem to have known which person was Jesus, Matthew ch.26 v.48; Mark ch.14 v.44; John ch.18 v.'s 4, 5).

The Messiah

The prophet Nathan told David his family line and kingdom would last forever. In the past God had told Moses that if the Israelites, his chosen people, obeyed, they would prosper.

So when they were conquered, the Israelites saw it as punishment for their sins – when they repented they would live in peace, wealth and glory under the rule of a Davidic king.

"…the people of Israel will have to live for a long time without kings or leaders… But the time will come when they will once again turn to the Lord their God, and to a descendant of David their king. Then they will … receive the Lord's good gifts" (Hosea ch.3 v.'s 4, 5).

The king was given the title of the Messiah (Hebrew, 'the anointed one'). In Greek it became 'Christos' and in English, 'Christ'.

Now and again the Israelites thought the Messiah had come, e.g. in the person of Zerubbabel, C.6th, following the exile. There is also the unidentified Messiah of "A child is born to us… he will be our ruler. He will be called, "Wonderful" … His royal power will continue to grow; his kingdom will always be at peace. He will rule as King David's successor, basing his power on right and justice, from now until the end of time" (Isaiah ch.9 v.'s 6, 7).

One conqueror, however, gave way to another (Assyrians, Babylonians, Persians, Greeks, Romans) and, to this day, Jews, in the religious sense of the word, still wait for their Messiah.

For Christians, Jesus is the Messiah. Hence, Jesus the Christ – Jesus Christ – Christians – Christianity. Traditionally, the church has taught a two-fold Messiahship: Jesus came as a servant and he will come again as a king.

The Temples in Jerusalem

Origins
The Tabernacle. A 'mobile' temple – a tent, about 60 feet long, 12 feet wide, 15 feet high, used by the Israelites during their journey from Egypt to Canaan (C.13th / C.12th).

The   Tabernacle

- The Holy of Holies → (upper chamber containing) ← The Ark of the Covenant
- The Holy Place →

King David wished to build a temple (2 Samuel ch.7 v.2). But God was content with a tent (2 Samuel ch. 7 v.'s 6, 7). Besides, David was a man of war who had spilt much blood (1 Chronicles. ch.22 v.8). His son, Solomon, would build the Temple (1 Chronicles ch.22 v.'s 9, 10; 2 Samuel ch.7 v.'s 12, 13). Nonetheless, David prepared materials for it (1 Chronicles ch.22 v.'s 2–5).

Solomon's Temple (about 950 B.C.)

In layout, similar to the Tabernacle, a Holy Place and a Holy of Holies, containing the Ark.

The basic building was about 90 feet long, 30 feet wide and 45 feet high. There were 3 storeys of rooms around it, possibly store-chambers.

The walls were lined with boards of cedar-wood with carvings of flowers, trees and cherubim; in the Holy of Holies there were two statues of cherubim, about 15 feet high; the Ark of the Covenant was beneath their outstretched wings.

"The whole interior of the Temple was covered with gold" (I Kings ch.6 v.22).

At the dedication, the building "was suddenly filled with a cloud shining with the dazzling light of the Lord's presence" (1 Kings ch.8 v.'s 10, 11). This temple was destroyed by the Babylonians in 587 B.C.

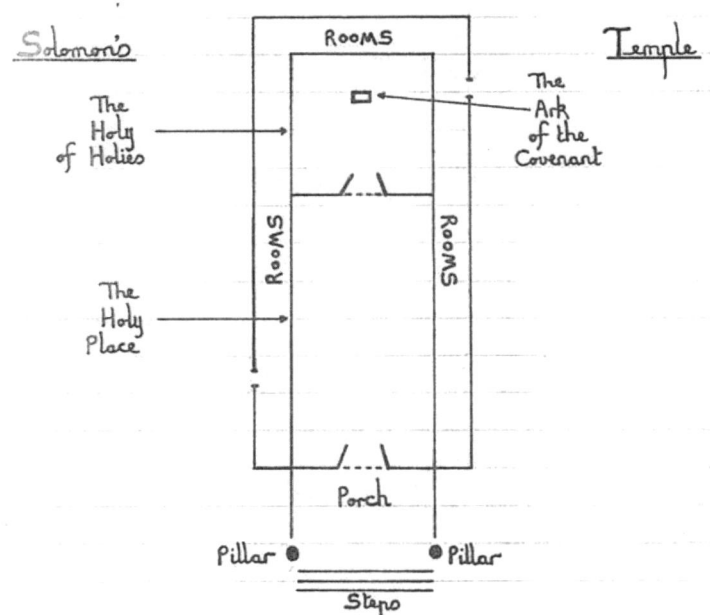

Zerubbabel's Temple (about 515 B.C.)

Under the governor, Zerubbabel, and urged on by the prophets Haggai and Zechariah, the exiles who had returned and the Jews who had remained built another temple.

According to a decree, it was to be 90 feet high and 90 feet wide (Ezra ch.6 v. 3). There were store-rooms and staff quarters.

The temple utensils (e.g. bowls and censers) taken by the Babylonians were returned, but the Ark of the Covenant had been lost.

This temple was defiled by the Greeks, who set up an altar to Zeus, cleansed and fortified by the Maccabees, but eventually captured by the Romans (63 B.C.).

Herod's Temple (begun, 19 B.C.)

The temple itself was completed within 10 years, but the surrounding area was extended and covered about 35 acres. Around the outer walls ran a covered arcade containing shops and schools. Here, sacrificial animals could be bought and money changed for the temple tax (see Mark ch.11 v.'s 15–17).

There were four courtyards – the Gentiles, the Women, Israel (the men) and the Priests. Within the Priests' Court was the Temple, consisting of a porch, the Holy Place and the Holy of Holies. Apart from the porch, which was 150 feet wide, the Temple was the same length and width as Solomon's, but three times higher. Like Solomon's, it had three storeys of rooms around it.

Parts of the outside were overlaid with gold. "…at the first rising of the sun it (the Temple) reflected back a very fiery splendour, and made those who forced themselves to look upon it, to turn their eyes away, just as they would have done at the sun's own rays. It appeared to strangers when they were at a distance, like a mountain covered with snow, for those parts of it that were not covered with gold were exceedingly white" (Josephus? Historian C.1st A.D.).

The Holy of Holies, empty and dark, was separated from the Holy Place by a curtain (see Mark ch.15 v.38).

This temple was destroyed by the Romans in 70 A.D. One wall still stands:

The Wailing Wall

Herod's Temple

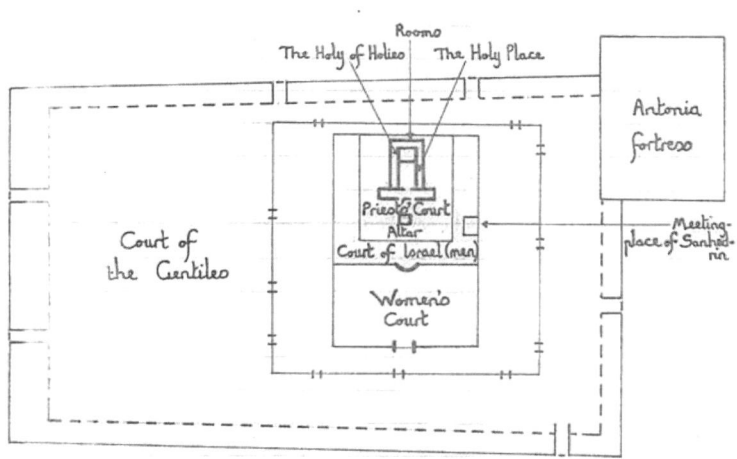

Today the temple area is dominated by a mosque known as 'The Dome of the Rock'.

Jerusalem, Dome of the Rock

Synagogues (meeting-places)

Like a church – services every Sabbath. But,

1. They were also used as town halls and schools.
2. They were administered not by priests, but by local elders – in particular, a chief officer (ruler) and his attendant.

It seems that synagogues were modelled on the Temple, and grew up during the Exile when there was no Temple.

There were synagogues throughout Israel, and wherever there were Jews (about 400 in Jerusalem!).

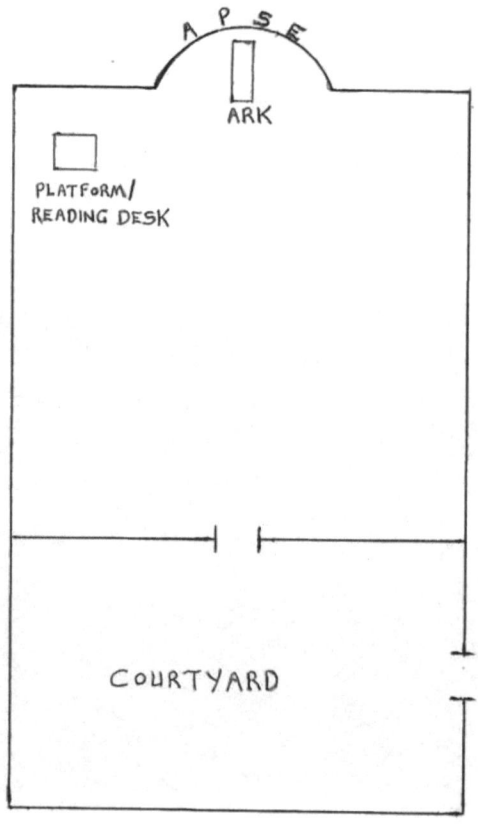

Illness (in biblical times)

There was a widespread belief that illness was a punishment for sin: God would not allow a person to suffer if they had not sinned. Jesus also implies this (paralytic by 4, Mark. ch.2 v.'s 1–12; the sick man at the pool of Bethzatha, John ch.5 v.'s 1–17, esp. v.14), though sometimes he suggests other causes, e.g. for the glory of God (the man born blind, John ch.9 v.1f., esp v.3), and, demon-possession (the blind and dumb man, Matthew ch.12 v.22 f., esp. v.28). It was "Satan" who had "kept bound up" the woman with a bent back (Luke ch.13 v.'s 10–17, esp. v.16). In every specific case of Jesus curing mental illness he drives out evil spirits (see, esp., Legion, Mark ch.5 v.'s 1–20).

With such a religiously-based view of illness it is probable that the sick commonly resorted to holy men / places. It was hoped that good-luck charms would keep the evil spirits at bay. There were doctors, but they are rarely mentioned. King Asa was criticised for turning to them and not to the Lord when he was crippled by a severe foot disease (2 Chronicles ch.16 v.12).

Medicines and oils were in use. Jeremiah refers to the "medicine" (balm) of Gilead (e.g. Jeremiah ch.8 v.22). The good Samaritan poured oil (and wine) on the wounds of the man who had been attacked (Luke ch.10 v.34). The only real prescription in the Bible, however, is "a paste made of figs", to put on a boil (2 Kings ch.20 v.7).

Broken limbs were tightly bandaged (compare swaddling clothes) and crutches may have been used.

The Bible, especially the Pentateuch, contains laws of hygiene (e.g. Deuteronomy ch.23 v.'s 12, 13; Mark ch.7 v.'s 3, 4,), and lists of clean food (e.g. Leviticus ch.11).

It does not record surgery, but at Lachish three skulls were found with holes bored in them, suggesting an operation to relieve pressure on the brain, perhaps to release demons.

Sacrifices – Offerings to God

In the Book of Leviticus, ch.'s 1–7, the following sacrifices are described:

Burnt:
Whole animal sacrificed. To take away sin (Leviticus ch.1 v.4) (though in 1 Samuel ch.6 v.'s 13, 14 offered at time of joy, and in 1 Samuel ch.13 v.'s 8, 9 in time of trouble).

Cereal:
Flour, olive oil and incense. A handful sacrificed; the rest for the priest.

Interpreted as remembering the worshipper to God.

In this section there is also the offering of the first corn harvested (Leviticus ch.2 v.12). (Compare the giving of the first-born, e.g. Exodus ch.13 v.15).

Fellowship:
Parts of animal sacrificed; the rest for the priest and any "clean" person.

"A thank-offering" (Leviticus ch.7 v.12), "in fulfilment of a vow" (Leviticus ch.7 v.16), a "freewill offering" (Leviticus ch.7 v.16).

Interpreted as a social, joyful sacrifice (1 Samuel ch.9 v.'s 12–26).

Sin:
    Unintentional, e.g. forgetting to make a religious payment.

    Intentional, e.g. stealing.

In some cases, whole animal sacrificed (e.g. Leviticus ch.4 v.'s 8–12); in most cases, part of it sacrificed, the rest for the priest (e.g. Leviticus ch.7 v.7).

Sacrifices have been seen as giving food to God (like a servant looking after his master), paying tax to him (the first-born), sharing a meal with him (compare the Passover custom of laying a place for "the stranger guest") and substituting one life for another (Lev. ch.17 v.11. Compare Lev. ch.16 v.21).

Frequently we are told God liked the smell (first mentioned Genesis ch.8 v.21).

Clearly different sacrifices had different purposes – to help take away sin (though there were many sins for which a sacrifice would not suffice, Numbers ch.15 v.'s 27–31. 1 Samuel ch.3 v.'s 13, 14), to show thanks, to pay dues and, simply, to give a gift.

QUIZ

PARTS OF A CHURCH

Match the words with their correct definitions:

1. Font — A room used to store the choir robes
2. Pews — The holy table, usually covered by a cloth
3. Pulpit — The part where the congregation worships
4. Lectern — A reading stand
5. Vestry — A basin used for baptism
6. Chancel — A platform used to deliver the sermon
7. Nave — Rows of seats
8. Altar — The part where the choir worships

SPELL THE FOLLOWING WORDS CORRECTLY

9. Israil
10. Pilat
11. Galillee
12. Salm
13. Isiah
14. Crucifiction
15. Jeruselam
16. Testemamt
17. Sakrifise
18. Ressurection
19. Eygpt
20. Frankinsence

NAME

21. Two sons of Adam.
22. One son of Noah.
23. Four sons of Jacob.

WHAT WERE THE FOLLOWING PEOPLE RE-NAMED

24. Abram?
25. Jacob?
26. Simon, son of John?
27. Saul?

WHAT WERE THE FOLLOWING PEOPLE NICKNAMED

28. James and John?
29. Thomas?

WHAT

30. Did God take from Adam to make Eve?
31. Stands today on the site of the Temple?
32. Is remembered at Whitsun?
33. Is the third of the ten commandments?
34. Article which may have been Jesus' is today in Turin cathedral?

WHAT ANSWERS WERE GIVEN TO THE FOLLOWING QUESTIONS

35. "Where will the Messiah be born?"
36. "Are you the Prophet?"
37. "So the girl went out and asked her mother, 'What shall I ask for?'"
38. "How much bread have you got?"
39. "Tell me, who do people say I am?"
40. "What, then, will the owner of the vineyard do?"
41. "Bring me a silver coin… Whose face and name are these?"
42. "Which commandment is the most important of all?"
43. "Are you the Messiah, the Son of the Blessed God?"
44. "What, then, do you want me to do with the one you call the king of the Jews?"

WHAT DO THE FOLLOWING WORDS MEAN

45. Christ?
46. Prodigal?
47. Gospel?
48. Apostle?
49. Covenant?

MOUNTAINS

Name the mountain on which,

50. Noah's ark lodged.
51. Moses received the Ten Commandments.
52. Moses saw the Promised Land.
53. King Saul died.
54. The prophet Elijah had a contest with the prophets of Baal.
55. Jesus ascended to heaven.
56. Abraham prepared to sacrifice his son, Isaac.

SEAS AND RIVERS

57. Name one river that flowed out of the garden of Eden
58. Name the river that Moses turned to blood.
59. What sea is also known as The Great Sea?
60. What river was Jesus baptised in?
61. What sea / lake did Jesus walk on?
62. What sea is about 1,300 feet below sea level?
63. What sea did the Egyptian army drown in?

WHO

64. Found himself in a valley covered with bones?
65. Was thrown into a den of lions?
66. Anointed David?
67. Killed more people at his death than during his life?
68. Climbed a tree to see Jesus?
69. Was given more wisdom than anyone before or after?
70. Ordered the death of John the Baptist?
71. Was released instead of Jesus?
72. Carried Jesus' cross?
73. Buried Jesus?

WHO SAID

74. "You are coming against me with sword… but I come against you in the name of the Lord Almighty…"
75. "All this I will give you… if you kneel down and worship me."
76. "And what is truth?"
77. "He will be called, Wonderful…"
78. "You are spies…"
79. "You have been so good to me, while I have done such wrong to you!"
80. "The woman… gave me the fruit, and I ate it."
81. "…three times I was whipped by the Romans…"

WHERE

82. Was the man journeying to when he was attacked by robbers in the parable of The Good Samaritan?
83. Did the son take his share of the inheritance to in the parable of The Prodigal Son?
84. Were the disciples when they were filled with the Holy Spirit?
85. Did Moses flee to after killing an Egyptian?
86. Was Saul / Paul journeying to when he was converted?

HOW LONG

87. Was Noah's ark?
88. Was the Ark of the Covenant?

HOW TALL

89. Was Goliath?
90. Was King Nebuchadnezzar's golden statue?

HOW MANY

91. Days in the story of Noah and the flood did it rain for?
92. Times did one of the disciples deny Jesus?
93. Times, altogether, did the Israelites march around Jericho?
94. Years did the Israelites wander in the wilderness?
95. Psalms are there in the book of Psalms?

HOW MUCH

96. Was Joseph sold for?
97. Was Jesus betrayed for?

WHAT ARE THE FOLLOWING COUNTRIES CALLED TODAY

98. Babylonia?
99. Persia?

100. A few words in the Bible include a 'double a', e.g. Naaman. Find 3 more.

ANSWERS

1. Font – a basin used for baptism
2. Pews – rows of seats
3. Pulpit – a platform used to deliver the sermon
4. Lectern – a reading stand
5. Vestry – a room used to store the choir robes
6. Chancel – the part where the choir worships
7. Nave – the part where the congregation worships
8. Altar – the holy table, usually covered by a cloth

9. Israel
10. Pilate
11. Galilee
12. Psalm
13. Isaiah
14. Crucifixion
15. Jerusalem
16. Testament
17. Sacrifice
18. Resurrection
19. Egypt
20. Frankincense

21. Cain. Abel. Seth.
22. Shem. Ham. Japheth
23. Reuben. Simeon. Levi. Judah. Issachar. Zebulun. Joseph. Benjamin. Dan. Naphtali. Gad. Asher.

24. Abraham
25. Israel
26. Peter
27. Paul

28. Boanerges – men of thunder
29. Doubting

30. A rib
31. A mosque (Mosque of Omar) (Dome of the Rock)
32. Pentecost – the apostles receiving the Holy Spirit
33. Don't misuse the Lord's name
34. His burial shroud.

35. In the town of Bethlehem in Judaea
36. No
37. The head of John the Baptist
38. Five loaves and also two fish
39. Some say that you are John the Baptist, others say that you are Elijah, while others say that you are one of the prophets
40. He will come and kill those men and hand the vineyard over to other tenants
41. The Emperor's
42. The Lord our God is the only Lord. Love the Lord your God with all your heart, with all your soul, with all your mind, and with all your strength.
43. I am, and you will all see the Son of Man seated on the right of the Almighty and coming with the clouds of heaven.
44. Crucify him!

45. The Messiah, The anointed one
46. Wasteful
47. Good news
48. Messenger
49. Agreement

50. Ararat / one in the Ararat range.
51. Sinai
52. Nego / Pisgah
53. Gilboa
54. Carmel
55. Olives
56. Moriah / one in the land of Moriah

57. Pishon. Gihon. Tigris. Euphrates
58. Nile
59. Mediterranean

60. Jordan
61. Galilee
62. Dead
63. Red

64. Ezekiel
65. Daniel
66. Samuel
67. Samson
68. Zacchaeus
69. Solomon
70. Herod (Antipas)
71. Barabbas
72. Simon of Cyrene
73. Joseph of Arimathea

74. David
75. Satan / The Devil
76. Pilate
77. Isaiah
78. Joseph
79. King Saul
80. Adam
81. Paul

82. Jericho
83. A country far away
84. Jerusalem / in one place
85. The land of Midian
86. Damascus

87. 133 metres (436 feet)
88. 110 centimetres (43-44 inches)

89. Nearly 3 metres (nearly 9.8 feet)
90. 27 metres (88.6 feet)

91. 40
92. 3
93. 13
94. 40
95. 150

96. 20 silver coins
97. 30 silver coins

98. Iraq
99. Iran

100. Baal. Aaron. Canaan.